STAY IN YOUR LANE

Table of Contents

INTRODUCTION

You've probably heard of the phrase "stay in your lane." And while we've all heard it shouted at us a few times by friends or family members while driving, it's also a very relevant phrase in life and business. Staying in your lane simply means sticking with what you know and with what you are good at. When is it appropriate to push the boundaries and try something completely wild and new? When should you stay in your lane? More often than not, it's helpful to leave the experimentation to others while you focus on your business and what you do best. "You gotta pick a path. And you gotta GO!"

As an entrepreneur, you're an expert (or an aspiring expert) in your field, but this doesn't necessarily mean you're great at everything. Nobody is. No matter how hard you focus on your business, there will be moments where you find yourself unprepared.

Successful business leaders spend their energy doing the things they already have a proven track record of succeeding in. If you do that, you can focus on your work and do the best job possible. Often, when small business owners overextend themselves, their businesses suffer. Have you ever seen a basketball player who tries to single-handedly carry a team when their teammates aren't pulling their weight? More often than not, the second half of the game exhausts them, and their team is still only a little bit closer to victory. Here are some more reasons you should stay in your lane to help your business stay on track toward success.

You've Surrounded Yourself with Pros

You should always surround yourself with good people. For example, when you interview candidates for jobs in your company, you should recognize where they excel and areas where they need improvement. If you can't do that right away, you probably have a good sense of it after a week or two. As a boss, it's your job to push people to greatness, but you should also allow them to excel where they're capable while you focus on your work.

PEOPLE+PROCESS+PRODUCT=SUCCESS

When You Don't Have to be Perfect, You Can be Good

When you accept that you aren't perfect at everything, you can focus on what you do better than anybody else. Take a moment to think of your shortcomings, but don't be too negative.

Considered one of the world's greatest minds, it was known to be highly disorganized. When you see where you need help, you can start hiring people to fill those roles. Or, maybe you already have someone on staff to help in those departments. Of course, when you stay in your lane, you should still be observing what's happening around you. It's essential to focus on your work, but don't lose focus on your business. Your employees may need to be guided back to their sweet spot every once in a while. When you need to make that correction, feel free to reference your limitations. Everybody has them.

Efficiency, Efficiency, Efficiency

One of the biggest hurdles small businesses have to overcome is workflow confusion; in other words, which employee should be working on specific jobs or tasks and when. When slip-ups like that happen, things fall through the cracks. Time is wasted. Potential earnings are missed. Tensions rise. Performance suffers.

A great example of this lesson was the owner of a 20-year old Illinois-based catering and food truck business.

From taking on many of his staff's responsibilities, it was clear that the owner was micro-managing his people in every facet of his business. In turn, this led to employee confusion as well as a lack of productivity and efficiency. Marcus helped the owner/operator rethink his responsibilities and the overall process and clearly define roles for each employee. So if you stay in your lane and focus on your work, and your employees know to stay in theirs, you can cut the confusion. When you focus on your business by tightening job scopes, your clear directions will be heard louder, and your productivity will rise.

When Traffic Makes You Change Lanes

In business, few rules can't be broken. As important as staying in your lane and instructing your employees to do the same, there will be times when you'll need to change course. Identifying those moments is difficult, especially if your head is down and all you do is focus on the work immediately in front of you. If you see employee satisfaction dropping, you need to make tweaks. No employee wants to feel like an insignificant cog in a company. By organizing a get-together once a month or so for your employees to socialize, you can bring together your team members who may not interact that often. Then, observe who is interested in what. Maybe the unhappy I.T. guy hangs out with the art department or marketing. That could be a passion of theirs that you didn't know about. Sometimes, when you focus on your work, you may miss your employees' hidden talents and skillsets. Even if your monthly pizza parties or donut breakfasts don't reveal crossover talents, it will still benefit you in at least two ways. First, these breaks contribute to employee satisfaction and retention. Second, you can introduce new ideas or products to your team to see what gets them excited. You can get opinions from trusted advisors throughout the organization, from the warehouse to the salesforce, making all team members feel valued and recognized.

You may need to rethink the "stay in your lane" mantra if your industry evolves because you will need to develop. "If you don't evolve, you will die." When all you do is focus on your current business model, you may be heading for disaster. That's not to say that you shouldn't focus on your work, just that there may be a time when your industry shifts and you need to break free from what you're doing.

When you stay in your lane and focus on your work, your goal is always ahead of you. You may face roadblocks that require you to take a different route than you imagined.

However, if you "Stay focused, work hard, know your numbers, and be disciplined," you can allow your team to focus on your business in their unique ways while you keep your company running at top speed and efficiency. The benefits of not overreaching are endless, and you will learn more about the employees you count on to make your journey as smooth as possible.

Power Of Positive Thinking

Always good to stick to what you are good at!!!

When it comes to building habits, the hardest thing for most people, including me, is sticking to it long enough for it to become ingrained.

Why don't we stick to a habit?

This is again a mind thing. The most common reasons people don't stick to a habit are:

- Habit is too tricky.

- You don't enjoy doing it.

- Too many patterns at once (habits are hard!).

- Too many other things are going on in my mind.

- When it's not routine (sick, travel, visitors, a big project at work).

- Not motivated to do it.

- You talk yourself out of it.

- You miss a day or two and get discouraged.

-

There are other reasons, too: people actively discourage you from changing, or you think negative thoughts about your ability to change, or you overdo it in the beginning and then run out of enthusiasm.

So how do we stick to a habit?

One Habit at a Time. This is incredibly important — most people ignore it because they underestimate how much focus it takes to stick to a new habit. It's easy to start a practice, or even 5 of them at once. Sticking to them is another story. Please note that this is one habit period — don't think you can make one fitness habit, one social habit, one work habit, etc. One habit only. Do not break this rule.

Focus on Starting. The only thing you need to do is start. If you're meditating, just get your butt on the cushion. If you're eating healthy, just bring your healthy snack (carrots & hummus?) in front of you, and take the first bite. If you're writing, close your browser, open a text document, and type the first sentence. Just start.

Enjoy Doing It. It would help if you got positive feedback for making the habit right away. Many people habitually hate built-in negative feedback and then wonder why they can't stick to it. Make a habit you love, or find a way to enjoy doing the practice. Could you focus on the positive aspects of it? I feel good about doing it. This is an immediate reward, and it's necessary.

Watch Your Thoughts. If you start to avoid the habit, make the habit but feel discouraged, or ever feel like quitting ... pay attention to these thoughts. Where are they coming from? Are you rationalizing quitting? Are you giving yourself some negative self-talk? Those thoughts aren't real — they're just defense mechanisms your brain uses to avoid discomfort. Let them go, and don't let them have power over you. You can beat them with some positive self-talk.

Be accountable. Tell at least one other person about your habit change, and ask them to keep you accountable. A group of 4-5 people is even better. It increases your likelihood of sticking to the habit by about 50%, in my experience.

Want to practice the habit rules by doing something crazily easy?

It will seem a little ridiculous, but spend a little time doing something stupid if you want to be good at it. Make the easiest possible habit when you first start.

Some ideas for habits to start with:

- Drink a glass of water each day.
- Put your clothes in your hamper.
- Wash your bowl when you're done.
- Say thank you every morning.
- Drink tea each afternoon.
- Eat one piece of fruit.
- Write one sentence a day.
- Floss one tooth.

Too easy? Try something more complex, and if you fail, then promise me you'll try one of these.

The Process Of Staying In Your Lane

This is it. The year you're going to stick to life changes. You set your resolutions and intentions for the year, and you're well on your way to accomplishing them. But you're starting to feel the pressure, or you're just waiting for the doom of that first slip up. Well, here are some ways to stick to the life changes you want to make.

1. **Determine why you want to stick to these life changes.**

Understanding why you do something is the key to sorting out how to do it. If you feel like your motivation is waning, it's probably because you're not clear why you're doing it. When you determine why you want to do something, decisions will flow, and you'll have a clear picture of the outcome. Set aside some time to consider your why, and don't settle for the first reason that pops up. The deeper you go, the more committed you will be to the work of sticking to the life changes you want to make.

2. **Make a plan of mini-plans.**

Once you're clear on why you won't stick to those life changes, you'll be ready to make a plan. Plus, you'll have a clear idea of focusing your energy to best support why you want to stick to your life changes. Use this newfound motivation to plan out your process step-by-step. You can start by brainstorming everything you will need to do and then list them out, week by week. When you break down your significant life changes into smaller goals, the pressure will ease, and you won't be so overwhelmed by the significant looming change you need to make.

3. Set attainable and measurable goals.

One of the most common reasons you don't stick to your life changes is because you're not setting attainable goals that you can track. Setting achievable goals isn't about selling yourself short, and tracking isn't about filling spreadsheets and graphs. You can accomplish almost anything you set your mind to with concrete steps that you can complete. So, dream big, but make sure your week-by-week goals are attainable within that time frame and are actionable rather than conceptual.

4. Set deadlines and stick to them.

Set mini-deadlines in your plan to stick to your life changes. Start from the final date you want to have accomplished your life changes and work backward from there. Ask yourself what you need to do each week to get yourself to that final destination.

5. Focus on the action rather than the goal.

To stick to your life changes, you need to focus on action. Don't get stuck setting mini-goals that rely on gaining rather than accomplishing. Gaining relies on outward forces while performing focuses on activities that you can achieve by your own volition. It would help if you addressed the how not the what.

6. Give yourself rewards and praise.

Are you waiting for your life changes to be a reality before you reward yourself? Huge mistake. Each step you take towards sticking to your life changes is a mini victory and deserves to be treated as such. A great and free way to reward yourself is through praise. Give yourself a fist pump, do a victory dance, or simply say sweet somethings of encouragement along your path to success. Bundle these mini-steps into more considerable strides and treat yourself with a greater reward for each set. This will make the road to that ultimate reward that much more pleasurable, not to mention motivating.

7. Track your progress.

One of the most effective forms of praise is to validate the progress you make by tracking the baby steps you take each day. Set up a neat chart or checklist that you can post on your desktop or bulletin board to remind you how stellar you are at sticking to your life changes. On your off days, look back at this progress for motivation and recognition.

8. Be present.

Sticking to life changes is a big commitment and becomes overwhelming very quickly. To ease the burden of change, be present. Focus on one task at a time and let yourself enjoy the process as much as you would the destination. When you feel stress and worry building in your head, bring awareness back to your breath so that you can have the most impact with each action you take.

9. Identify what's holding you back.

A lot of people are afraid of success. Counterintuitive, yes, but true. Face your fears and challenges, don't ignore them. Identify what's holding you back, then make a list of ways you can overcome those challenges. It may be fear, a lack of support from your family, or it may be that you haven't identified you're why. Whatever it is, don't let it hold you back just for lack of awareness.

10. Visualize your progress.

Visualizing your success keeps you motivated and focused. Take it a step further by visualizing your progress. Imagine yourself doing the work it takes to stick to life changes. This practice mentally prepares you for the effort to stick to life changes and helps surface any challenges or even tools you may have overlooked.

11. Have fun.

Sticking to life changes doesn't have to be boring. Incorporate some fun into your tasks to make the journey worthwhile. Use a playlist of your favorite songs, go outside, be silly. Channel your inner eight-year-old to find creative ways to make your action plan action-packed.

12. Let your goal evolve.

You learn and grow every day, so why shouldn't your goals also evolve with you? The life changes you set out to make may take drastic turns or slight transitions. You're not failing when you let your goal develop; you're growing and setting yourself up for tremendous success. Sticking to life changes isn't about checking off a list; it's about embodying your desires and dreams.

13. Remember, it's not all or nothing.

The journey is as much an accomplishment as the destination. Treated as such, you won't need to stick to life changes because you'll be living them day to day.

Failure Is A key To Finding Your Lane

The 3 Stages of Failure in Life and Work (And How to Fix Them)

One of the hardest things in life is to know when to keep going and when to move on.

On the one hand, perseverance and grit are vital to achieving success in any field. Anyone who masters their craft will face moments of doubt and somehow find the inner resolve to keep going. If you want to build a successful business or create a great marriage or learn a new skill, then "sticking with it" is perhaps the most critical trait to possess.

On the other hand, telling someone never to give up is terrible advice. Successful people give up all the time. If something is not working, intelligent people don't repeat it endlessly. They revise. They adjust. They pivot. They quit. As the saying goes, "Insanity is doing the same thing over and over again and expecting different results."

Life requires both strategies. Sometimes you need to display unwavering confidence and double down on your efforts. Sometimes you need to abandon the things that aren't working and try something new. The critical question is: how do you know when to give up and when to stick with it?

One way to answer this question is to use a framework I call the 3 Stages of Failure.

The 3 Stages of Failure

This framework helps clarify things by breaking down challenges into three stages of failure:

Stage 1 is a Failure of Tactics. These are HOW mistakes. They occur when you fail to build robust systems, forget to measure carefully and get lazy with the details. A Failure of Tactics is a failure to execute a good plan and a clear vision.

Stage 2 is a Failure of Strategy. These are WHAT mistakes. They occur when you follow a strategy that fails to deliver the results you want. You can know why you do the things you do, learn how to do the work, but still choose the wrong what to make happen.

Stage 3 is a Failure of Vision. These are WHY mistakes. They occur when you don't set a clear direction for yourself, follow a vision that doesn't fulfill you, or otherwise fail to understand why you do the things you do.

Fixing a Failure of Tactics

A Failure of Tactics is a HOW problem. In Centratel's case, they had a clear vision (to be "the highest-quality telephone answering service in the United States") and a good strategy (the market for telephone answering services was significant). Still, they didn't know how to execute their strategy and vision.

There are three primary ways to fix Failures of Tactics.

- Record your process.
- Measure your outcomes.

- Review and adjust your tactics.

Record your process.

Whether running a business, parenting a family, or managing your own life, building great systems is crucial for repeated success. It all starts with writing down each step of the process and developing a checklist you can follow when life gets crazy.

Measure your outcomes. If something is important to you, measure it. If you're an entrepreneur, measure how many sales calls you to make each day. If you're a writer, measure how frequently you publish a new article. If you're a weightlifter, count how often you train. If you never measure your results, how will you know which tactics are working?

Review and adjust your tactics. The fatiguing thing about Stage 1 failures is that they never stop. Tactics that used to work will become obsolete. Tactics that were a bad idea previously might be a good idea now. You need to be constantly reviewing and improving how you do your work. Successful people routinely give up on tactics that don't move their strategy and vision forward. Fixing a Failure of Tactics is not a one-time job; it is a lifestyle.

Fixing a Failure of Strategy

A Failure of Strategy is a WHAT problem. By 1999, Amazon had a clear vision to "be earth's most customer-centric company." They were also masters of getting things done, which is why they were able to roll Amazon Auctions out in just three months. The why and how were handled, but then what was unknown.

There are three primary ways to fix Failures of Strategy.

- Launch it quickly.

- Do it cheaply.

- Revise it rapidly.

Launch it quickly.

Some ideas work much better than others, but nobody knows which ideas work until you try them. Nobody knows ahead of time—not venture capitalists, not the intelligent folks at Amazon, not your friends or family members. All of the planning and research, and design is just pretext.

Do it cheaply.

Assuming you have achieved some minimum level of quality, it is best to test new strategies cheaply. Failing cheaply increases your surface area for success because it means that you can try more ideas. Additionally, doing things cheaply serves another crucial purpose. It reduces your attachment to a particular concept. If you invest a lot of time and money into a specific strategy, it will be hard to give it up on that strategy. The more energy you put into something, the more ownership you feel toward it. Bad business ideas, toxic relationships, and destructive habits of all kinds can be hard to let go of once they become part of your identity. Testing new strategies cheaply avoids these pitfalls and increases the likelihood that you will follow the plan that works best rather than the one you have invested in the most.

Revise it rapidly.

Strategies are meant to be revised and adjusted. You'd be hard-pressed to find a successful entrepreneur, artist, or creator who is doing precisely the same thing today as when they started. Starbucks sold coffee supplies and espresso machines for over a decade before opening their stores. 37 Signals started as a web design firm before pivoting into a software company worth over $100M today. Nintendo made playing cards and vacuum cleaners before it stole the hearts of video game lovers everywhere.

Too many entrepreneurs think if their first business idea is a failure, they aren't cut out for it. Too many artists assume that if their early work doesn't get praised, they don't have the skill required. Too many people believe if their first two or three relationships are wrong, they will never find love.

Imagine if the forces of nature worked that way. What if Mother Nature only gave herself one shot at creating life? We'd all just be single-celled organisms. Thankfully, that's not how evolution works. For millions of years, life has been adapting, evolving, revising, and iterating until it has reached the diverse and varied species that inhabit our planet today. It is not the natural course of things to figure it all out on the first try.

So if your original idea is a failure and you feel like you're constantly revising and adjusting, cut yourself a break. Changing your strategy is expected. It is the way the world works. You have to stay on the bus.

Because of this, it is critical to launching strategies quickly. The faster you test a system in the real world, the quicker you get feedback on whether or not it works.

Fixing a Failure of Vision

A Failure of Vision is a WHY problem. They happen because your vision or goal for what you want to become (you're why) doesn't align with your actions.

There are three primary ways to fix Failures of Vision.

- Take stock of your life.
- Determine you're non-negotiable.

- Navigate criticism.

Take stock of your life. People rarely take the time to think critically about their vision and values. Of course, no requirement says you must develop a personal vision for your work or life. Many people prefer to go with the flow and take life as it comes. In theory, that's just fine. But in practice, there is a problem:

If you never decide on a vision for your life, you'll often find yourself living someone else's dream.

Adopting someone else's vision as your own—whether it be from family, friends, celebrities, your boss, or society as a whole—is unlikely to lead to your dream. Your identity and your habits need to be aligned.

Because of this, you need to take stock of your life. What do you want to accomplish? How do you want to spend your days? It is not someone else's job to figure out the vision for your life. You can only do that. My suggestion is to start by exploring your core values. Then, review your recent experiences by writing an Annual Review or doing an Integrity Report.

Determine you're non-negotiable. Your "non-negotiable" is the one thing you are not willing to budge on, no matter what.

One common mistake is to make your strategy non-negotiable when it should be your vision. It's straightforward to get fixated on your idea. But if you're going to get obsessed with something, get obsessed with your image, not your opinion. Be firm on the vision, not on this particular version of your idea. "We are stubborn on vision. We are flexible on details."

The key is to realize that nearly everything is a detail—your tactics, your strategy, even your business model. If your non-negotiable is to be a successful entrepreneur, there are many ways to achieve that vision. If Amazon's non-negotiable is to "be earth's most customer-centric company," they can lose billions on Amazon Auctions and Amazon zShops and still reach their goal.

Once you are confident in your vision, it is rare to lose it in one fell swoop. There are so few mistakes that lead to the destruction of a dream. More likely, you failed at a strategy level and felt demoralized. This crippled your enthusiasm, and you gave up not because you should but because you felt like it. Your emotions caused you to turn a Stage 1 or Stage 2 failure into a Stage 3 failure. Most of the mistakes that people assume are Failures of Vision are Failures of Strategy. Many entrepreneurs, artists, and creators get hung up on a particular version of their idea, and when the assertion fails, they give up on the vision as well. Don't develop a sense of ownership over the wrong thing. There are nearly infinite

ways to achieve your eye if you are willing to be flexible on the details.

Navigate criticism. Criticism can indicate failed strategies and tactics, but—assuming you're a reasonable person with good intentions—it is rarely an indicator of a failed vision. If you are committed to making your dream a non-negotiable factor in your life and not giving up on the first try, then you have to be willing to navigate criticism. You don't need to apologize for the things you love, but you do have to learn how to deal with haters.

The 4th Stage of Failure

There is the 4th stage of failure that we haven't talked about: Failures of Opportunity.

These are WHO mistakes. They occur when society fails to provide equal opportunity for all people. Failures of Opportunity result from many complex factors: age, race, gender, income, education, and more.

For example, there are thousands of men my age living in the slums of India or the streets of Bangladesh who are more intelligent and more talented than I am. Still, we live very different lives mainly because of the opportunities presented to us.

Failures of Opportunity deserve an article of their own, and there are many things we can do as individuals and as a society to reduce them. However, I chose not to focus on them here because Failures of Opportunity are difficult to influence. Meanwhile, your vision, your strategy, and your tactics are all things you can directly control.

A Final Note on Failure

Hopefully, the 3 Stages of Failure framework has helped you clarify some of the issues you're facing and how to deal with them. One thing that may not be apparent at first glance is how the different stages can impact one another.

For example, Failures of Tactics can occasionally create enough havoc that you mistakenly believe you have a Failure of Vision. Imagine how Sam Carpenter felt when he was working 100 hours per week. It would have been easy to assume that his vision of being an entrepreneur was a failure when, in fact, it was merely poor tactics causing the problem.

Sometimes you need a few tactics to create enough whitespace to figure out your strategy or vision. This is why I write about how to manage your daily routine, figure out your priorities, and why multitasking is a myth. No, these topics aren't going to create a world-changing vision by themselves. But they might clear enough space in your calendar for you to dream up a world-changing idea.

In other words, you might not be walking the wrong path after all. It's just that there is so much dust swirling around you that you can't see the way. Figure out the right tactics and strategy—clear the dust from the air—and you'll find that the vision often reveals itself.

Five ways the best leaders learn from failure

Wildly successful people have incredible stories of failure and have generously and courageously shared them with the world. While their circumstances differ significantly, the thread that joins them is that loss made each person stronger.

Our most successful leaders are those who can learn and grow from these experiences. Yet dealing with failure well is not a skill we are ever taught how to do. It is a skill we either learn the hard way or not at all.

Considering the importance of this skill to our future success, personally and professionally, below are five ideas to help us learn and grow stronger from failure.

1. Start seeing success and failure as two sides of the same coin. There is a tendency to attribute success to our brilliance and failure to external factors (e.g., other people, luck, timing, environment, market conditions, etc.) when, of course, both success and failure are caused by a combination of our brilliance – or lack thereof – as well as various external factors. Examining both internal and external antecedents opens up the possibility for more learning.

The complexity of our work means just about everything we do – whether it is raising a child or delivering a product to a client – will have elements of both success and failure. Yet, human tendency towards bifurcated thinking has us labeling them as one or the other. Under examination, success and failure start to look a lot alike, so we should, as Rudyard Kipling suggests, "meet with Triumph and Disaster, and treat those two impostors just the same."

2. Avoid the error of attributing blame to the first reasonable factor. It is more likely many interrelated issues are at play. Most failures are worth discussing the result from layers of decisions and actions based on assumptions, beliefs, personalities, etc. When things do not go as planned, it is worth taking a few moments to consider all the reasons why.

Deepening our understanding of the sequence of events leading to past failure makes it obvious we had multiple opportunities to stop it, and therefore, various ways of preventing similar errors in the future. Asking "why?" five times is a popular technique used to think through some of these root causes and is valid as long as the focus is on building our understanding of how we contributed to the failure instead of finding someone or something to blame.

3. Take the time to turn individual learning into tangible changes and improvements. Many organizations have processes in place to learn from failures. You may call them after-action reviews, post mortems, or something else entirely. Still, all too often, the learning achieved through these processes is not translated outside of the meeting room or pages of the lessons learned report. Investing time in education is commendable but ultimately useless unless it leads to changes that prevent the error in the future.

Whatever learning process you use should lead to a list of action items that include timelines and accountability checks. The action items do not have to be set in stone; they should adapt as you learn what works and what does not. The point is to make it easy to translate learning into organizational change. Otherwise, your hard-earned lessons sit on a shelf, collecting dust.

4. Do not fall prey to lose aversion. It is well known we feel the pain of loss more than the satisfaction of gains, even when they are quantitatively equal. In an organizational context, that intense pain of loss when we try something that does not work can cause us to pull back, stop taking risks and give excuses to stick with the status quo.

Protecting our ability to take risks and innovate requires changing how we relate to the experience of failure. Instead of focusing on the loss, we have to frame each failure as an opportunity to accelerate our learning and become better and more robust in the long run. The best organizations at this start by preparing everything they do as experiments where the goal is learning.

5. Be smart about how you invest time and resources in learning. No one wants to go through an intensive, organization-wide after-action review when the situation is better suited to a quick conversation with a colleague. Conversely, if other people need to understand the failure to avoid making similar mistakes, the learning should not happen behind closed doors. Pick a process that is appropriate for the scale and type of the loss.

The four ideas listed above apply regardless of the scale. This last idea simply asks you to consider the causes and the consequence of the failure. A failure caused by incompetence looks very different than a failure caused by experimentation. In the former, learning might focus on an individual's capacity; the latter might look at evolving the experiment. Similarly, understanding the consequences makes a massive difference in how we deal with a failure and should help us determine how many and which people to involve in the learning process and how to turn that learning into change, and eventually, success.

Overcoming Adversity

Adversity is a state of hardship, difficulty, or misfortune that one deals with in life. One can face six types of adversity, and facing adversities in life can break or make a person. It may lead one person to improve their life by finding ways around their challenges, or it may lead another person to turn to drugs or alcohol to lessen the psychological toll that their hardships cause.

The Types of Adversity

1. Physical Adversity

Physical disability is an example of physical adversity. For example, a professional athlete may face physical adversity after experiencing a career-ending injury, drastically changing their life trajectory. Furthermore, being blind, deaf, obese, or in chronic pain and having to deal with the difficulties of those ailments may force someone to fight to achieve an everyday life.

2. Mental Adversity

A mental problem, or mental illness, may limit someone. Seeking help from a doctor, psychologist, or psychiatrist can significantly improve one's life when dealing with mental adversity. Enhancing one's well-being and achieving an everyday life are the goals of seeking treatment.

3. Emotional Adversity

Emotional maturity allows us to have a productive state of mind and face difficulties in life. Self-worth is vital to develop, as rage and sadness can lead to dealing with daily life problems. We need to control our emotions so they do not control us.

4. Social Adversity

Social interaction is crucial to human life. Being limited in social skills can severely limit a person from getting a job, making friends, or maintaining a family unit. Developing these skills can significantly improve one's life.

5. Spiritual Adversity

Faith in a higher power does not have to be a God, but faith is an advantage in life. It helps when one has hope, compassion, and love for themselves and others to cope with daily life.

6. Financial Adversity

This may be the most apparent adversity that our society and the rest of the world faces. Not being able to afford necessities creates a barrier to leading a happy life and jealousy and anger.

No matter the type of adversity you are experiencing, our Fort Behavioral Health team provides comprehensive therapeutic programs to give you the mental strength you may need. Also, the enhanced self-confidence that you may feel after your therapy sessions will provide the foundation for future success. Also, you will gain skills and strategies that will help you continue to conquer adversity when it appears in your life.

7. Defeat Adversity with Help from Fort Behavioral Health

Everyone faces adversity in life, just at varying degrees and in different contexts. You can take steps to deal with your particular hardships or misfortunes and turn negative issues into positive life paths. Dedication, motivation, and belief in oneself are vital to improving our life circumstances, regardless of our adversities.

If you are struggling with life's hurdles, and are experiencing a subsequent addiction to drugs or alcohol to cope, understand that you are not alone, and there is hope for a better future.

Tips For Overcoming Adversity

Anyone who has ever achieved something worthwhile has had challenges and setbacks – because anything worth doing will be complicated. Overcoming adversity is a necessary step on the road to greatness.

"He that wrestles with us strengthens our nerves and sharpens our skill. Our antagonist is our helper." Life is the worthy opponent – the antagonist – we all need to grow. When you have the right tools for how to overcome adversity, you're able to embrace it as a helper instead of letting it stop you from achieving your goals.

1. Be Prepared

You can work on overcoming adversity before it even happens. Train your brain to be resilient by building your inner strength and developing a growth mindset. Examine your limiting beliefs to uncover what's holding you back. Develop a support system that you can fall back on. When the time comes to dig deep and discover how to overcome adversity, you'll be prepared.

2. Practice Positivity

How does a person overcome adversity? It's often about the way they frame the things that happen to them. Take a step back and positively reframe the problem. Catch negative self- talk and replace it with empowering beliefs that help you work toward your goal rather than undermine it.

3. Stay Disciplined

When tough times hit, it can feel like your life is out of control. That's why rituals are a powerful tool for overcoming adversity. When you create positive habits like priming, meditation, and daily exercise, you're preparing your mind and body for trouble. Sticking to a daily routine through good times and bad will bring order and empowerment to your life.

4. Stay Focused

Getting what you want in life is all about focus. No matter what happens, you must keep your eye on the prize. Remember why you wanted your goal: it's your purpose, passion, and reason for living. Visualize your life when you've achieved your dreams. Stay focused on your ultimate goal, no matter what. There's no room for self-pity and no time for negativity when you're learning how to overcome adversity.

5. Find The Lesson

Realizing that life happens for you, not to you, is key to overcoming adversity. Every event in your life can teach you something. Those who can find the lessons will succeed. Those who blame their circumstances on others will fail. Take responsibility. Evaluate what happened and why. Determine how you can prevent it from happening in the future. Then move on.

6. Work On Your Skills

The most outstanding leaders and most successful people know that there is always room for improvement. "If you're not growing, you're dying." Overcoming adversity is about taking an honest look at your knowledge and skills and working to improve them every day. Work on your public speaking. Become a better networker. Improve your understanding of finances or management. You'll feel more confident and prepared for the future.

7. Get Inspired

To answer the question, "How do people overcome adversity?" go to the source. Read the biographies of people who have achieved what you want in life. From Oprah Winfrey to Bill Gates, there's no shortage of real-life examples of overcoming adversity. Need a quick pick-me-up? Find inspirational quotes to post on your mirror or fridge. Proactively feed your mind, and you'll change your entire state.

8. Elevate Your Peer Group

Looking to success stories can help you learn how to overcome adversity – but you must also look at those around you. "The quality of a person's life is most often a direct reflection of the expectations of their peer group." You are who you hang out with. And if you want to bounce back from challenges, live optimistically, and stay focused, you need to surround yourself with people who support you – not people who hold you back.

9. Get A Coach

Overcoming adversity takes just the right blend of positivity and realism, of passion and real-life skills, of inner strength and an external support system. A results coach can help you balance it all and stay on track. They're professionally trained in the art of overcoming adversity. They can give you the mix of guidance, goal-setting, and tough love you need to get through tough times and come out the other side stronger and wiser.

10. Don't Give Up

"Persistence overshadows even talent as the most valuable resource shaping the quality of life," Surfer Mick Fanning got back on his surfboard just six days after a shark attack. Stephen King's classic novel Carrie was rejected 30 times. Thomas Edison tried thousands of methods before making a successful lightbulb, saying, "I have not failed. I've just found 10,000 ways that won't work." That's a perfect way to sum up how to overcome adversity.

Keep Your End Goal In Mind

Keep your end objective in mind means being mindful of your end goal when doing something. There are two steps to it:

First, be clear on your end objective.

Second, evaluate your actions against this objective.

1. Be clear on your end objective

There are three kinds of end objectives you need to be clear on:

Life objective: What is your life purpose?

Goal objective: What is the aim of your goal?

Task objective: What is the aim of this task you are doing?

Each objective sets the context for the things that follow. Your life purpose determines what you do in your life and the goals you set. Your goals determine the tasks and things you do daily. And your studies determine what you spend time on. This means that the jobs you do every day should be a subset of your goals, while your goals should be a subset of your life purpose.

Your life purpose is like your ultimate objective in life. If you are unclear on your life purpose, the other things that follow will be ambiguous. While you can be pursuing goals, they may or may not lead you to your ultimate destination when you're 50, 60, 70, or 80 years old.

Similarly, if you are unclear on your goals, your day-to-day tasks will be random and, at times, directionless. While you can be busy every day, you will often find that you've not accomplished much at the end of the month, three months, or six months. At the end of this is a busy but unproductive and unfulfilling life.

When you have your life objective and goal objectives clear, you will identify your task objectives too clearly.

2. Evaluate what you're doing against this objective

Different obstacles will start emerging in your path as you pursue your objectives with everything in life. Multiple options start getting dangled in front of you, each with its own set of pros and cons. Forks in the road appear. Different considerations start seeping in. As if that isn't enough, people start giving their own opinions and take on your situation. In no time, you start becoming confused by everything that is before you.

When that happens, just recall what your end objective is – the very same objective you identified in the beginning. Assess everything that you see against it. Evaluate your options in terms of how well it serves your objective. If you find that the option does not meet your objective, throw them away. You will discover that decision-making becomes condensed into an effortless and straightforward task.

Ways To Stay Focused In A World Full Of Distraction

In every success story, the longest chapter is the one about determination.

While success demands many things from us, willpower and determination always come up at the top of the list. Many people believe that we are born with determination, and those who succeed are simply the fortunate ones born with an abundant supply. But if you ask any successful person, they will tell you they were not born with more determination; they always found a way to harness and use what they have more effectively.

Here are five ways to harness your determination and stay focused:

1. Set Up Your Day The Night Before

Before you go to sleep, make some fundamental decisions about what you will do tomorrow, such as what you will wear, what you will eat for lunch, and the route you will take to work. It is easier to pack a healthy lunch the night before than to decide what you will have with a hot dog vendor parked in front of your workplace.

The same applies when it comes to spending money. Decide on a budget and stick to it.

Make a decision the night before that you won't check your emails or surf the net before you have finished the more critical tasks that need to be completed. Stick to your schedule, and at the end of the day, close your eyes for a few minutes and take in how good you feel to be in charge of your day.

Getting into the habit of planning your day will remove your easiest decisions from the table, making it easier to avoid getting sidetracked and wasting time and energy on small, unimportant things.

2. Do The Most Difficult Things First

The most challenging duties will not get easier the more we fret about them or put them off. We will only waste energy that would be better spent by just digging in. Get after the most challenging job right away while you are still fresh and have the power.

Our minds are sharpest in the morning, which is when we should tackle the tough jobs. After these are out of the way, we can relax and take care of the more routine work that doesn't require much in the form of mental strain, ability, and energy.

3. Eliminate Distractions And Time Wasters

Real emergencies will come up, and we have to deal with them. The majority of situations that do come up to distract us are not emergencies and do not require us to respond right away. Many of these situations will resolve themselves on their own with time.

Responding to these requests immediately will only set you

up to receive more. By not responding, you are sending a message that you are a strong-willed, focused person who is very busy, and over time, you will be bothered less by trivial, time-wasting matters.

4. Regenerate And Keep Up Your Energy

Take a quick break when working on something if you feel your energy fading. Take a brisk walk, run, stretch, or do whatever results in you taking a brief retreat from work and regenerate. You will come back to your task with renewed vigor and a sharper mental focus.

Instead of eating a large meal at lunch, snack on healthy foods such as fresh fruit and vegetables during the day. Drink lots of water and get into a regular exercise program. Arrange a routine with these matters so that you don't have to think about them; they just become part of your daily regime.

5. Constantly Remind Yourself Of Your Ultimate Goals

Create a vision board, a mind movie, or some system that serves as a constant reminder of what you are working toward. The "why" behind the goal is crucial as it will serve as a motivator.

Suppose you want to earn $10 million to start a school in a third-world country. Have a clear vision of what the school would look like to imagine it regularly. Set aside average time daily, if only five minutes, to visualize this goal. The more details you can put in, the better. Become emotionally involved with the visualization by putting music, videos, or anything that provides you with an emotional charge. The emotional connection is hugely important, as this will motivate you to keep moving toward your goal.

How to Overcome the Most Common Obstacles That Prevent People From Living Their Dreams

No matter what kind of goal someone is trying to reach-- health, financial, parenting, relationship, or career--some common traps might keep them from living their dreams.

Here are the most common traps that could prevent you from reaching your goals and the strategies that will help you avoid them:

1. Putting your goals off until 'someday.'

Since 'someday' never appears on the calendar, you'll never accomplish your goals if you keep pushing them off. The best of intentions won't do you any good without a clear plan.

Solution: If a goal is essential to you, create a timeline. Even if you can't start working on it today, at least tell yourself when you can tackle it. Whether you want to apply for promotion once your child starts school or you plan to return to college when you turn 40, stop using the word 'someday.'

2. Waiting to take action until you 'feel' ready.

If you wait until you feel ready to tackle something challenging, you might be waiting a long time. It's unlikely that you're going to gain a sudden burst of inspiration out of the blue.

Solution: Change your behavior first. Sometimes, the emotions change later. Take action, and you may gain the ambition you need to keep going.

3. Not anticipating the tough times.

Whether you want to get out of debt or you're hoping to lose weight, change isn't easy. You'll encounter some days that are harder than others, and it's essential to accept that there will be a rough road ahead.

Solution: Think about potential pitfalls you might face and develop a plan for dealing with those times when you might be tempted to give up. When you have a plan, you'll feel more confident in your ability to keep going.

4. Viewing mistakes as failure.

Progress rarely comes in a straight line. But sometimes, people think one step back means they've gone back to square one, which causes them to give up.

Solution: Recognize that you're going to mess up sometimes. But rather than declare yourself a dismal failure, use your energy to create a plan to get back on track.

5. Not making your goal a priority.

It's easy to say you want to change, but doing the work is much different. You have to decide what kind of priority you're going to give your goal. Otherwise, your intention will get lost in all your other daily activities.

Solution: Identify one step you're going to take every day and put it in your calendar. You're more likely to go to the gym, apply for a job, or spend one hour researching your new business idea if you establish a time to do it.

6. Underestimating how hard it will be.

Tackling a new goal is easy but sticking to it is hard. Assuming, "This won't be a problem at all" can leave you unprepared for the reality of the situation.

Solution: Don't confuse overconfidence with mental strength. Rather than tell yourself it's going to be easy, remind yourself you'll need to work hard to achieve your goals, despite whatever skills and talents you already possess.

7. Giving up before you see results.

Impatience is the enemy of change. And in today's digital world, most people struggle to wait for the time it takes to reach a goal.

Solution: Just because you can't see results doesn't mean your efforts are wasted. You need to stick to your goals longer than you might think before you experience lasting change.

8. Sabotaging yourself just before the finish line.

The fear of success can be a real problem. And if you're not careful, you might sabotage yourself before you reach your goal. Perhaps you don't believe you're worthy of success, or maybe; you are afraid someone will take it away from you.

Solution: Think about past goals you've struggled to reach or those you've failed to attain. Be honest about your feelings, and be on the lookout for warning signs that you might be throwing in the towel.

9. Setting your sights too high.

If you're excited about changing your life, you might be tempted to set the bar high. If you take on too much too fast, however, you'll set yourself up for failure.

Solution: Focusing too much on a big goal can be overwhelming. Establish short-term objectives and celebrate each milestone along the way.

Tips To Stay On Top Of Your Goals

Ever set goals and then let them slide to the bottom of your list? Here are tips to help you stay on top of your goals and finally build your dream life.

When you're setting your goals, the secret to success is to prioritize the vital few and not take on more than you can chew. This makes progress achievable, which fuels your motivation to continue.

You must set goals the right way and make sure you track them. But what's the secret to accomplishing the goals that you set?

To accomplish what you set out to do, you must keep your goals top of mind!

Once you've figured out what you want and why you want it, the next step is to remind yourself of that vision.

When you're slogging through a crappy commute to an awful cubicle, keep your goals top of mind.

When you're overwhelmed by the amount of stuff you need to get done around the house, keep your goals top of mind.

Keep your goals top of mind when you're struggling to pay your bills and budget your money.

Write them down every day

Writing your goals down on a piece of paper repeatedly is much more powerful than thinking about them once in a while in your head.

Writing those ten dreams down every morning keeps your vision front and center. You know what you want, and you don't stray.

The focus for today ensures that you are actively moving toward one of your goals. Every day matters and should bring you closer to your dream.

The gratitude practice ensures that we remain optimistic about all of the things we already have. It keeps us from only seeing the gap.

STOP SCROLLING!

Take action: grab a journal or any old piece of paper, and write down the answers to the above statements. Do it right now! And then keep doing it tomorrow.

Join a butt-kicking, goal crushing, accountability group

I can't put enough emphasis on the importance of surrounding yourself with people that are going to lift you!

It's hard enough to chase our dreams when we're filled with our self-doubt. It's damn near impossible when other people are shooting down our goals and dragging us to the bottom with them.

Find a group of people that will listen to your goals, encourage you to pursue them, and hold you accountable to your commitments, and your success will skyrocket.

Having a safe place to state your goals and knowing you have to follow up on your progress makes it hard to forget about what you set out to do. It's a great way to keep goals top of mind.

Put up a motivating vision board

You can think about your goals, but that's not nearly as powerful as writing them down.

You can write your goals down, but that's not nearly as powerful as seeing them.

Whether you use a bulletin board, a bristol board, a piece of paper, or the front of your fridge, put up some pictures of what your life will be when you achieve your goals.

The magic happens when you see those images, and you get a tiny glimpse into the world where you've finally succeeded.

When you can feel the feels that come with hitting your

goals and reaching your dreams, all of a sudden, you're not going in the cookie jar, you're not choosing Netflix over your side hustle, and you're not putting up with what your mother thinks about you buying a tiny home.

Put together a vision board for ten years from now, one year from now, or even just one goal from now—something to remind you why it matters so much.

Create mini reminders with sticky notes

A vision board sounds fantastic and looks great on Pinterest, but it can also be a little intimidating.

If a vision board is not your cup of tea, another great way to keep your goals top of mind is to use sticky notes all over your home.

You can write your goal to build six-pack abs and stick it on your remote control.

You can write your goal to stay off social media and stick it on your laptop.

You can write your goal to eat whole foods and stick it on your pantry.

It may sound silly to put sticky notes everywhere, but keeping your goals top of mind is a massive factor in your success. If you can make your goals pop out wherever you are, you'll be more likely to stick to them.

Use that thing in your hand

Unfortunately, we spend more time than ever holding on to and checking our phones these days. What if every time you touched your phone, you were reminded of your goals?

You'd fit in so much extra inspiration into your day.

Put a motivational quote that is related to your goal onto

your lock screen.

Use the background to remind you what your goal is, whether through pictures or words.

Set the alarm or a reminder to review your goals or work on your dreams at a particular time each day.

Since we are so connected to our devices, this is a great way to make our phones work for us by helping to build our dream lives.

Time block goals in your bullet journal

Big lofty dreams are fantastic for thinking outside of the box and shooting for the stars. However, goals still need to be broken down into manageable chunks so that you can take action and move toward success.

If you 'time block' actions in your bullet journal (or any planner that you use), you will have a reminder every day of your goal and your next step to achieve it.

This will help keep it top of mind, and it will help you get it done.

Don't just write a list of 'to dos' down the side of your page. Take the time to schedule specific hours where you will be able to devote the time to make things happen, or else it won't...

Implement an effective goal setting routine

Implementing a process or a routine for reviewing your goals and setting new ones allows you to ensure you're heading in the right direction.

You can see whether you're actioning things at a good pace or not, and you can adjust to make sure you hit your goal for the year.

When goals are part of your monthly/weekly/daily routine, you consistently keep them top of mind.

The more regularly you review your goals, the more natural it becomes to check in on your intentions for the month and see how you're performing against them.

A good goal routine is pivotal in keeping you on track to hitting your goals and living your best life.

Track your progress

If you can't see the progress you're making toward your goal; it is so easy to forget about your intentions and to give up.

Seeing the small wins getting you closer to the end will remind you why you started in the first place.

Tracking your progress through apps, habit trackers, or sticky notes — whatever method works best for you — allows you to keep your goals top of mind and keep your motivation sky high.

Celebrate small wins

When you hit a mini-milestone in your journey, it is so important to celebrate it!

Dreams are big.

Goals are hard.

Giving yourself the credit you deserve — when you've stuck it out in the gym every morning for a week, or surpassed a record running time you hadn't hit before, or did a public speech for the first time, or finished a race you've never done before, or didn't yell at your kids all morning — these are things that need to be acknowledged!

You don't have to spend all your money on a fancy dinner

and undo the healthy eating habits you've been working to maintain, but you do need to take a few minutes in the day and just grin with pride that you're finally doing it.

You're finally getting closer to your dream.

Consume related media

With the crazy amounts of information available to anyone and everyone on the internet today, it is easy to become dissuaded.

Suppose your goal is to declutter your whole house and downsize to a tiny home this year. In that case, your mountain will get bigger and bigger every time you see Pinterest and Facebook and Instagram images of your friends with their mansions in gated communities.

Consume content that aligns with the values you have for your life.

Read blogs where people are doing the exact thing you want to do.

Stay off Facebook if all your 'friends' are doing the exact opposite.

Watch YouTube videos of how it's done.

Read books about people that are doing what you want to do.

Find a tribe that shares your passion.

Setting goals is the more specific component of personal development.

We generally know the things we'd like to improve and the direction we want to head in.

Although we might not dare to dream too big from the start, we tend to have an idea of the life we want to live.

Are you achieving goals? That's when things get complicated.

Our lives are already so busy that it's easy to let things slip to keep all the balls in the air.

The key to successfully achieving your goals is to get crystal clear on the critical few actions and keep them top of mind every day.

Keeping A Positive Mindset On What You Want From Life

Maintaining a positive attitude is critical when you want to achieve anything or simply improve the quality of your life. Most successful literature will talk about the power of positive thinking and its importance, but it's often easier said than done.

Here are some tips for maintaining a positive attitude no matter what's going on in your life.

1. You Determine Your Reality

It's important to realize that you determine your reality by the way you react to the outside world. When something happens, you get to choose whether it's a positive or negative situation and respond accordingly.

For example, if you lose your job, your first reaction will likely be one of anger, frustration, and hopelessness. However, what if you could turn those emotions around and look at that experience as an opportunity.

You now have the chance to find a job where you will learn new skills and perhaps even be happier. And in the meantime, you have some free time to analyze what direction you want the next stage of your life to go in.

2. Start Your Day Strong

Most people have to drag themselves out of bed, which sets a negative state of mind for their entire day. Positive people create a long-term morning ritual that reinforces how great life is and how happy they are to be alive.

Whether you have 1 minute, 15 minutes, or an hour to dedicate to your ritual, you can start the day in a way that helps you feel relaxed and ready for the day ahead.

3. Exercise Is the Natural Feel-Good Drug

Exercise is a great way to maintain a good attitude because of all the positive chemicals it releases into the bloodstream.

One study found that between groups who participated in high-intensity interval training, moderate continuous training, and no exercise, those in the second group experienced the most significant drop in depressive symptoms and stress. Therefore, if you're looking to exercise to help you feel good, get your heart rate up, but don't push too hard, or you may increase overall stress.

Also, remember that exercise can include many activities. If you don't like running, try dancing or kickboxing instead. Put on some upbeat music to kick up the positive vibes even more.

4. Use Books, Audio, and Videos to Overload Your Brain with Positivity

There are millions of excellent books, podcasts, and videos for you to absorb from people who are inspiring and living the life of their dreams. Tap into their positive emotions and experience by learning how they think and what they do to create the lives they want.

You can do this in the morning or while exercising, eating, commuting, cooking, cleaning… there's always time for positivity.

5. Your Language Shapes Your Thoughts

Minor changes in your language can change the way you think and how you act. Whenever someone greets you and asks how you're doing, do you answer with "fine" or "not too bad"?

Think about just what this language is communicating to others… and yourself.

I always answer with "great," "fantastic," or "amazing." Not only does this remind me that life is excellent, but it usually helps the other person shift toward a positive attitude as well.

Also, take some time to look at the way your inner voice talks to you. Is that language positive or negative? If it's overly critical or negative, it may be time to tap into some mindfulness meditation to shift your inner critic to an inner cheerleader.

6. Hang out With Positive People

You will often have a similar level of health, income, and lifestyle as the five people you spend the most time with.

So if you want to be fit, then start to hang out with healthy people. Want to start a business? Then hang out with business owners. And if you're going to be positive, make sure you're hanging out with positive people.

7. Show Your Appreciation for Others

By appreciating others for a job well done, outfit, or smile, you start to cause a positive chain reaction. Stop complaining and focus on all the good others are doing around you.

Don't you feel great when you receive a compliment from someone else? If you want to receive more, then start giving them out and watch what happens to the people around you.

One particular study found that people who sent letters of gratitude experienced significant increases in happiness scores. If you don't feel like writing a letter, send an excellent text to someone who recently helped you out, or send an email thanking your coworker for always helping pick up the slack around the office. Whatever it is, take some time to show gratitude.

8. Garbage In, Garbage Out

This is an expression from programming where the result is only as good as the input. If you're feeding yourself with negativity all day long, then it's pretty obvious you're going to be feeling negative as well.

A great deal of the media thrives on negativity. Put yourself on a harmful diet (including people) and watch how easier it is to maintain your positive attitude.

9. Stop Negative Thoughts in Their Tracks

It's hard to be a constantly positive person, and negative thoughts will bubble up from time to time. These will be more frequent initially but can decrease as you practice the tips we're talking about. When you notice negative thoughts, you can use a pattern interrupt to stop them in their tracks.

The idea is to interrupt your current thought pattern and shift to a more positive outlook. One way to do this is to set a visual or auditory cue. It can be something as simple as a bracelet you wear each day or the sound of a car passing outside your window. Whenever you see or hear the cue, use it to shift your thoughts to something positive.

10. Live With Gratitude

So many positive things happen during our day, and we often ignore them while letting one negative comment or event ruin our mood. It can help keep a gratitude journal where you jot down things you are grateful for each night or during the day.

If you're reading this, then you probably live with a roof over your head and food in your belly, which is a daily struggle for a large portion of the world. However, we often take these things for granted and don't realize how great we have them.

Try refocusing your thoughts towards everything you do have instead of what you don't. One study found that reflecting on past experiences with a sense of gratitude can increase hope and happiness. That's a great reason to give it a go today.

You can find more ways to practice gratitude in this book.

11. Recharge Your Batteries

One key to adopting a positive attitude is taking the time to recharge your batteries. This might mean taking a few hours on the weekend to read a positive book or taking a few weeks for a holiday. It will help recharge your motivation in life.

If you're not in the position to travel, you can take a staycation or have a "home holiday" where you simply switch off from the outside world and spend time doing things you love.

Final Thoughts

You now have these tips for maintaining your positive attitude, but they are no use to you unless you implement them into your life.

Start small, pick the most straightforward tip that you love, and introduce it into your life starting right now. Then, over time, start implementing the other recommendations and watch your positivity soar.

How to Think Positive and Eliminate Negative Thoughts

In a world full of external factors that we cannot control, it is becoming more and more important to at least maintain ourselves.

Thinking positively can have a tremendous effect on our lives. By eliminating negative thoughts, we can influence the part of our lives at least that we can control: our mindset.

When you're currently surrounded with negativity – whether that's because of a stressful project or problems in a relationship – you should try to dissect that challenge into different sub-challenges.

For example, if you have to deliver a huge presentation at work on Friday, try to think of this enormous task as multiple smaller tasks:

- Find sources to support your presentation

- Think of exciting anecdotes, introductions, or examples

- Create a general outline of your presentation

- Complete the first five slides

- Add a small video or puzzle to your presentation

- Finish the presentation

- Think of a keyword for each slide to remember what you have to say

- Practice the presentation to finish it within 30 minutes

- Deliver a great presentation

While this example may not be relevant to you, the message is all the same. You can tackle pretty much any obstacle – no matter how big it may seem – as long as you take it one step at a time.

That's how you can eliminate negative thoughts such as "I can never do that" or "I'll never be good enough" or "I'll never reach that goal" from controlling your actions.

Take it one step at a time, and pretty much any goal becomes manageable.

Step 2: Realize That Positive Thoughts Can Be a Choice Happiness is determined as follows:

- 50% is determined by genetics

- External factors determine 10%

- Your outlook defines 40% Numerous researchers have studied this determination, and while the details differ, the results all share the same observation:

- Your thoughts can influence your happiness.

Even though there are things in life that we cannot control, we can still often influence how we react to these things.

In that sense, we might not get to control 100% of our happiness, but we can still influence a big chunk of it.

I believe we can learn to influence the 40% of our happiness determined by our outlook. Happiness is a choice, and you can learn to recognize these situations on your own.

How does this help you to think positively and eliminate negative thoughts?

Well, because this shows you that it pays off to learn how to think positively in difficult situations.

By developing this skill, you can increase happiness in your life. It is not always easy, but you can change a bad day into a good one by focusing on the positives instead of the negatives.

Step 3: Spend Time with the People That Have a Positive Influence on Your Life and Be Grateful for Them

Almost everybody has a small circle of people they trust and love, whether a partner, family, or friends. These people have a positive influence on your life.

I want you to focus on spending more time with these people. When surrounded by negativity, you are more likely to postpone activities that require you to be outgoing. You'd rather be lazy and watch Netflix all day than go outside and meet up with your friend.

You must try to break out of your comfort zone and spend more time with those who positively influence your happiness. These people can act as a support net for the moments when you're feeling down. This might sound intimidating and scary, but it's a step that should not be underestimated.

Even when you don't feel comfortable sharing your challenges with these people, there's another thing you can actively do to initiate positive thoughts; and that's to be grateful that these people are in your life:

Be thankful that you have parents who support you, no matter what you do.

Be thankful for the friends with whom you can laugh your

ass off.

Be grateful that you have a healthy and loving partner.

Be thankful that you have a kid that looks up to you and thinks you are the best.

Being grateful might sound like a rather pointless thing to do. Why would being grateful help you in thinking more positively and eliminating negative thoughts?

Well, the answer is simple.

Being grateful forces you to think of the good things that you already have in your life. This allows you to face your issues with optimism instead of negativity. People that actively practice gratitude are much better able to deal with toxic emotions.

So what do you have to do?

Go out there and meet up with the people you love, and be grateful for having these people in your life.

Step 4: Don't Give up After a Setback

So you had a bad day last week? Or maybe a terrible week in which you allowed negative thoughts to control your life? Who cares!

We are only human, so we're bound to experience a day of negativity every once in a while. It's important to realize that everybody occasionally shares negative thoughts in their life. Eternal happiness does not exist. Even the happiest man alive has experienced negativity and sadness on some days.

What you need to do when this inevitably happens to you:

- Don't let this set you back.

- Don't interpret it as a failure

- Don't let it stop you from trying to think positive

You see, even the most optimistic person experiences negativity on occasion. Sure, we can try to be as positive as possible every day, but we have to accept that negativity is something we have to deal with from time to time.

So what if you're engulfed in negative thoughts today? Screw it and know that tomorrow is a new day and that you can try to work on this again.

Here's no arguing that we cannot control 100% of our happiness. We can't stand in front of a mirror, repeat the words "I am thinking happy thoughts only" ninety-nine times and accept to be happy suddenly.

It doesn't work like that.

However, there are several things we can do to at least improve our mindset when we get to choose how we react to external factors.

I hope that you have a better idea of what you can do in these situations. Sooner than later, you will influence your mindset to think positively and to eliminate negative thoughts.

Having Definite Goals And Affirming Them

Why You Must Have a 'Definite' Goal to Become Successful

Many people drift through life not knowing where they're going. They don't even know where they want to go or what they want to do in the first place.

If you don't know where you want to go, you can take any road — any road will take you anywhere. When you don't have a clear picture of the ultimate goal on your mind, it's easy to go everywhere but where it matters.

If you want to become successful in life, you must have a definite goal — where you want to go, what you want to become, where you want to see yourself in the future. A definite purpose will help you with keeping you focused on the work that matters most.

Have the big picture in mind

The great danger for most of us lies not in setting our aim too high and falling short, but in setting our aim too low and achieving our mark.

Your work gets easier when you see the big picture. It

makes it easy to divide your work into small chunks and work for the small wins that accumulate into your enormous success, eventually.

The big picture tells you where you want to see yourself in the future. Ask yourself where you want to be in five or ten years. Make this future you "the" person you admire.

Make a checklist of habits your future self would possess. Think about what you would be like in the future — how you would behave, what you would do to make you successful, etc.

Follow this checklist religiously. Make "your future self" your hero. You want to be like him. He's everything you ever wanted to become.

This checklist will help you make sure you're doing everything your future self would do — everything that made him successful. Make these habits part of your everyday life. With the day-to-day practice, make them your own.

Make decisions based on where you want to go

If you don't know where you are going, you will probably end up somewhere else.

Most people can't think outside the box. They keep them inside the shells. They can't get out of their head and think through. They set their goal based on their current status.

If you set your goal based on your present self — your current abilities — you'll settle for a life of mediocrity.

Set your goal based on where you will be when you become successful. This way, you'll have set yourself a goal to become the best version of yourself.

You're not successful for a reason — you need to prepare yourself to handle success. When you work hard to succeed, you achieve the finest qualities — persistence, focus, discipline, perseverance — needed to deserve success. Without these qualities, you're not ready for success yet.

You lack one or more of these qualities in your present condition. So if you set a goal based on your present situation, you won't be able to develop a bigger plan because you know your current state — you know what you can do and can't do.

If you think through and see the big picture instead, you'll set yourself a goal based on where you will be. You'll have a plan that will eventually turn you into "the person you admire."

It gets easier to find something when you know what you're searching for

First, have a definite, clear, practical ideal; a goal, an objective. Second, have the necessary means to achieve your ends; wisdom, money, materials, and methods. Third, adjust all your means to that end.

Your work gets easier when you know what you want, and you know you need only that thing. When you're searching for a needle in the haystack, you set your focus on finding the needle. You're digging through the haystack, but what you need is the needle — not the haystack.

The same goes for personal goal setting. When you want to become successful at whatever you want to do in life, you need to have a definite goal on your mind. You must know what you want and how to get it.

If you don't know what success means to you or what you want to be, you will go nowhere with your life — you will stay right where you are in life.

If you want to become successful — as you're reading this

book, I'm assuming you want it badly — set your goal first. Then make strategies to get there. This is the first step towards success. Nonetheless, the most crucial part of your journey towards success.

Getting success is no easy feat, but you can make it easier by setting the goal first. Once you have a definite plan in place, achieving success will get easier.

Having a definite goal ensures you're on track to become successful. If you don't have a well-defined plan, you won't become successful. Period.

Sit quietly and think through. Listen to your heart — but be rational in your thinking. Ask yourself what you want. There you have your goal when you get the answer. Now all you have got to do is make your dream come true.

Why Setting Clear and Definite Goals Is Important

Imagine you could choose three wishes to be granted; what would you choose?

Would you ask for the first thing that comes to your mind, or would you give the matter some deep thought and make a wise choice?

Maybe you know exactly what you want, and you don't even have to think about it.

If you are clear about your goals, this is easy. However, if you don't know what you want, this is a difficult question.

Most people don't have clear goals. However, if you want to achieve success in your life, you need to know precisely what you want. Without setting clear and definite plans, you will not focus your energies and will not accomplish much.

How to Set a Clear Goal

If you want to succeed, you need to set goals. Without goals, you lack focus and direction. You might start a project, quit it, and start something else. This leads nowhere.

Your first step to success should be to know precisely what you want.

You must have clear goals. Why? Because a clear plan is the shortest path to realizing it.

This is a difficult task for most people. Many go through life where it takes them, lacking any direction. They find it difficult to arrive at a clear understanding of their abilities, what they are best suited to do, and what they desire to do with their lives.

It would help if you looked inside you for the answer.

Sit down every day, with a pencil and paper, where you won't be disturbed, and write down all the ideas that come to your mind.

Analyze every desire. Find its pros and cons, and whether you want it achieved. You will be surprised how many ideas, which look plausible at first, become unimportant goals after a bit of thinking.

Set attainable goals. Make sure that it's possible to achieve the goal you set and that you want to accomplish it. If you set unrealistic goals or ones you do not wish to, you will waste time and energy.

Don't despair if you don't find anything that interests you. Just keep thinking, writing down, and analyzing your ideas day after day.

Even if you don't find what is most essential for you to after a few days, a week, or more, the understanding and insight will gradually unfold.

After going through the above steps, sift the goals you thought about, and make a priority list.

Write down the most important goals, and look at this list every day, several times a day.

Now, with an open mind, start thinking about what could be the first step to take toward success.

Remember, even small goals are goals.

One of the reasons people find it challenging to decide about goals is because they believe they have to choose something big, which frightens them. They might be afraid of the significant responsibilities that come with pursuing and achieving big goals and prefer to lead a simple, ordinary life.

When looking for your true desires, don't just think about the wealthy and famous people you see on TV or read about in the newspapers. Though people might like to see them and read about them, not everyone wants to attain fame and power.

This might seem strange to say, but most people would feel more comfortable and satisfied with smaller goals.

Achieving smaller goals on a personal and more mundane level might be what you want or prefer, and that's quite okay.

Questions to Ask Yourself about Your Goals

Ask yourself the following questions about your goals:

- Upon achieving this goal, would I be happy and satisfied?

- What will it solve in my life?

- What will be its effect on my life?

- What will be its effect on other people?

- Do I want to achieve this goal?

After finding what you want, and are sure about it, try to see how you can make your goal a little bigger.

Don't limit your thinking because whatever the mind can conceive and believe, it can eventually accomplish. For example, if your goal is finding a good and satisfying job, think about something more significant and believe you can get it.

If you desire a certain amount of money and feel mentally comfortable with it, try thinking about a more significant amount.

If your goal is to lose a few pounds, try getting your mind comfortable with the idea of losing a little more, provided, of course, you don't harm your health.

After setting clear and definite goals, you will certainly know what your three most important wishes are.

You don't need to ask for a genie to grant your wishes because you have within you the power to make them come true. These are the powers of visualization and affirmations.

Remember, what the mind can conceive and believe to be possible, it can eventually achieve.

Tip 1

Frame your goals in positive words. Look at your goals as realistic and achievable, no matter how big they are.

Tip 2

Build a realistic mental image in your mind with all the details. This would help you pinpoint all the details. The clearer your goal is, the easier it would be to achieve it.

How Do Positive Affirmations Work?

People often ask about affirmations, how to use them, and whether they work.

They ask, "Do affirmations work?"

"How affirmations work?"

I am sure you have heard about affirmations. In case you didn't, affirmations are positive statements, which describe in positive words the desired situation, event, habit, or something that we want to possess or achieve.

Do Affirmations Work?

If you ask whether affirmations work, the answer is yes, they do. To make them work, you have to repeat them often, attentively, while believing that what you are affirming is either already confirmed or in the process of becoming true.

Gradually, as you repeat the positive statements – positive affirmations, they sink into the subconscious mind and influence it to act by the repeated words.

As you repeat the words with belief and focus, your motivation and desire grow more robust and push you to start taking action to make the words you are repeating come true.

You will begin to think positively and to expect success.

You will begin to recognize opportunities when they appear. Gain new friends or meet people who would help you.

Find the right book, information, advice, or guidance that you need.

You will also find solutions to problems and answers and insights related to the goal you want to achieve.

If you wish to get results to repeat Affirmations often

How to Get Results with Affirmations

The words that you often repeat in your mind ultimately affect your subconscious mind and reprogram it according to the idea and terms of the affirmation. By repeating the affirmations, you program your subconscious mind to help you manifest your goals, change your habits or develop new skills.

It is not enough to repeat affirmations just a few times. This is one of the reasons for the failure to get results, which eventually leads to losing faith in the promises and stop using them.

If you wish to use these positive words and statements and get results, it would be good to start with small goals at first to get some experience. This will also show you, first hand, how they work so that you can use them better.

Starting small also gives you the faith and confidence you need when working on bigger goals.

It often happens that after a few days of repeating affirmations, the mind starts raising doubts about the efficiency and usefulness of the commitments, and you start asking yourself whether affirmations do work at all.

If your goal is minor, it takes a shorter time to achieve it, and therefore, the mind has less time to raise doubts and neutralize your efforts. This is another reason why it is better to start small.

Small success at first will strengthen your faith in the method, and your mind's resistance will get weaker.

How Do Affirmations Work?

Again to the question, "Do affirmations work?" Yes, they do if you use them correctly.

What Affirmations Do?

Repeating affirmations motivates you to act to attain your desire or goal.

By repeating affirmations, you become aware of opportunities that might surface, making your aims and goals come true.

Affirmations strengthen your ambition and desire.

The words you repeat get engraved on your subconscious mind and affect behavior and habits.

They program the subconscious mind to bring up helpful ideas and solutions.

Affirmations activate the power of the subconscious mind, which will supply the desire, ideas, opportunities, and even the right circumstances.

To produce results with affirmations, you need to repeat them often, with attention, interest, and desire, and add emotions and inner conviction.

Be careful not to weaken them by raising doubts and thinking negatively. It is a waste of time to repeat them and then doubting their efficiency.

It is also essential that you don't just repeat the words, stay passive and wait for results to appear out of thin air. You need to follow your intuition, open your mind, seize opportunities that come your way, and take action.

Positive affirmations, together with positive actions, produce results.

If you repeat negative words and repeatedly think about problems and obstacles, you are signaling to your subconscious mind that it is difficult to make positive changes in your life.

On the other hand, if you are positive and constantly repeat positive words, you will ultimately shape your life by these words.

Now, to the question, "do affirmations work" they do but don't take my word for it. The best way to answering this question is to try them for yourself. Just learn more about them, follow the instructions, and see for yourself.

The techniques for following them are pretty simple. You can use affirmations to achieve goals, and you can also use them to improve your daily life for encouragement, inspiration, and motivation.

Sometimes results are almost immediate, and sometimes they take time. This depends on your goal, dedication, efforts, and other factors.

They do work if you use them correctly, which is not a difficult thing to do.

Here are a few examples:

"I am attracting happiness and joy into my life."

"I am becoming a friendly person, and I am attracting new friends to me."

"I have found a wonderful and well-paying job." "My life is improving day by day."

"I have a wonderful and satisfying job."

"I have money in my bank account and feel financially secure." "I am going to get excellent grades at the examination."

"I think positive thoughts that attract happiness and prosperity into my life."

"Happiness is welling from inside me day and night."

If you wish to learn more about affirmations, how do they work, and how to use them effectively to make changes in your life, get a new job, earn more money, change habits, or for anything else, you will find the book "Affirmations Words with Power" most helpful.

You will find in this book all the techniques, instructions, and advice that you need, as well as affirmations for almost every purpose and goal.